SOUP

EASY RECIPES FOR
EVERY OCCASION

ALEX RAY

summersdale

SOUP

Summersdale Publishers Ltd
46 West Street
Chichester
West Sussex
PO19 1RP
UK

www.summersdale.com

Printed and bound in Malta

ISBN: 978-1-84953-813-8

Substantial discounts on bulk quantities of Summersdale books are available to corporations, professional associations and other organisations. For details contact Nicky Douglas by telephone: +44 (0) 1243 756902, fax: +44 (0) 1243 786300 or email: nicky@summersdale.com.

CONTENTS

Hearty soups

Fancy soups

> **STOCKS ARE THE BEDROCK OF GOOD SOUP. THERE'S NO DOUBT THAT STOCK CUBES AND POWDERS ARE USEFUL AND CONVENIENT, BUT WHEN YOU TASTE THE DIFFERENCE IN THESE MADE-FROM-SCRATCH STOCKS, YOU'LL AGREE THAT THEY'RE DEFINITELY WORTH THE EFFORT.**

BASIC
STOCKS

VEGETABLE STOCK

This simple vegetable stock will enable you to create tons of tasty homemade meals. Once it's frozen, you'll have a secret shortcut to dozens of delicious dishes.

Makes 1.2 litres

Ingredients

4 medium carrots

2 large onion

2 celery stick

12 black peppercorns

2 dried bay leaves

6 fresh parsley stalks

(A bouquet garni can be used if fresh herbs are not available)

Preparation method

Peel and roughly chop the carrots, onion and celery, then put all the ingredients into a large pan and cover with water.

Bring to the boil. Cover and simmer very gently for 30 minutes.

Strain into a large bowl and allow to cool.

Use within three days or freeze.

If you do plan to freeze, reduce the stock by half by boiling vigorously, then allow the liquid to cool.

Pour into ice cube trays and freeze. Once frozen, the cubes can be placed in a labelled bag and stored for up to three months.

Tip

A range of other vegetables can be used in this stock, according to taste, e.g. broccoli, cabbage, etc.

CHICKEN STOCK

The perfect way to polish off Sunday's roast chicken – have this herby stock on hand and you're halfway to dinner before you've started!

———— Makes 750 ml–1.25 litres ————

Ingredients

1 large carrot

1 large onion

1 celery stick

Bones from a leftover roast chicken carcass

6 black peppercorns

1 dried bay leaf

3 fresh parsley stalks

1 sprig fresh thyme

(A bouquet garni can be used if fresh herbs are not available)

Preparation method

Peel and roughly chop the carrot, onion and celery, then put all the ingredients into a large pan and cover with water.

Bring to the boil and skim off any scum that has formed. Cover and simmer very gently for 2–3 hours.

Strain into a large bowl and allow to cool. Chill overnight.

Skim off any fat that has formed on the surface. Use within three days or freeze.

This method gives a real depth of flavour and, like the vegetable stock (above), it's a useful ingredient to have on standby, so freezing's a good idea.

To do so, reduce the stock by half by boiling vigorously then allow the liquid to cool. Pour into ice cube trays and freeze.

Store in the same way as the frozen vegetable stock cubes on page 9.

BEEF STOCK

A deep, rich stock that will add intensity to any meat dish.

——————— *Makes 1.5–2 litres* ———————

Ingredients

1 kg beef bones
3 onions
2 carrots
2 celery stalks
2 leeks
2 ripe tomatoes
Salt and pepper

Preparation method

Preheat the oven to 200°C.

Cut the onions, leeks and tomatoes into quarters and the carrots and celery into large chunks.

Use leftover bones (including marrowbones) or buy from your butcher. If the bones are large, ask the butcher to chop them into smaller pieces. Put the bones in a large roasting tin together with the onion, carrots, celery and leek and roast for 30 minutes until starting to brown (check regularly to ensure the bones aren't burning).

Tip the bones and vegetables (including all the brown bits from the bottom of the tin) into a large saucepan and add the tomatoes and enough cold water to cover everything.

Bring to the boil, cover, then simmer for at least 3–4 hours (the longer the cooking, the richer the stock). If the water level drops and no longer covers the bones and vegetables you may need to top it up - it's worth checking regularly. Remove any scum or foam as needed.

Season and then strain using a fine sieve.

Store in the same way as the frozen vegetable stock cubes on page 9.

"

SOMETIMES SIMPLE IS BEST. VEGETABLES ARE THE PERFECT BASE FOR MANY DELICIOUS AND STRAIGHTFORWARD SOUPS. THESE RECIPES ARE PROOF THAT QUICK AND EASY *DOESN'T* MEAN COMPROMISING ON FLAVOUR.

"

SIMPLE VEGETABLE SOUPS

BROCCOLI SOUP

When you've five friends arriving for dinner in half an hour, an ambitious main to be assembled and a three-tier confection cooling in the fridge, whizz up this easy-to-make bowlful and rest assured your starter is a triumph.

———————————— *Serves 4–6* ————————————

Ingredients

1 large onion

3 medium potatoes

750 g broccoli

2 tbsp cooking oil (vegetable or olive)

1.2 litres vegetable or chicken stock

Salt and pepper

Preparation method

Peel the onion and potatoes. Chop the onion finely and the potatoes into chunks along with the broccoli.

Heat the oil in a large saucepan on a medium heat.

Add the onions and gently fry for 3 minutes until softened then add the broccoli and fry for a further 5 minutes, stirring all the while.

Add the potatoes, stock and season to taste.

Bring to the boil, then simmer on a lower heat for 20 minutes until the vegetables are soft.

Remove from heat and leave to cool, then blitz until smooth. Season to taste.

Reheat gently for 5 minutes before serving.

Tip

To make it a bit more dinner-party-esque, add a swirl of double cream before serving.

TOMATO AND BASIL SOUP

Morecambe and Wise, fish and chips, tomato and basil.
Some things are just meant to go together.

———— | *Serves 4* | ————

Ingredients

1 kg ripe tomatoes
3 garlic cloves
Small handful of basil leaves
1 tbsp extra virgin olive oil (plus more to serve)
600 ml vegetable stock
Salt and pepper

Preparation method

Preheat the oven to 190°C.

Cut the tomatoes in half and place cut side up in a
roasting tin.

Peel and slice the garlic.

Keeping 4 leaves for the garnish, rip up half of the basil and scatter on top with the garlic.

Sprinkle with the olive oil and roast in the oven for 15–20 minutes, until the tomatoes are soft.

Blend the tomatoes, garlic and basil (and their juices) with the stock and the remaining basil until smooth.

Reheat gently, adding salt and freshly ground black pepper to taste.

Chop the four reserved basil leaves finely and use to garnish the soup, along with a swirl of olive oil.

Tip

If you want to make the soup go further, simply add a tin of chopped tomatoes before blending.

MUSHROOM SOUP

Rich, earthy and very, very simple.

———————————— ⊣ *Serves 4* ⊢ ————————————

Ingredients

1 medium onion
Knob of butter
1 tbsp olive oil
1 garlic clove
450 g mushrooms
1 medium potato
750 ml vegetable or
  chicken stock
Salt and pepper

Preparation method

Finely chop the onion. In a large saucepan melt the butter
with the oil and fry the onion until soft and translucent.

Peel and crush the garlic, stir into the onions and cook
for a further minute.

Roughly chop the mushrooms, add to the pan and cook for around 5 minutes, stirring regularly.

Peel and chop the potato and add along with the stock.

Bring to the boil before reducing the heat and simmering until the potato is cooked through (around 25 minutes).

Blend and season to taste.

Tip

Use a mix of fresh wild mushrooms – available in many supermarkets – for a more intense flavour. If you prefer a creamier soup, stir in 100 ml of crème fraiche to the hot soup before serving.

SPICY SQUASH SOUP

The perfect warmer on a chilly day, this is the culinary version of a cosy blanket. But much easier to eat.

 *Serves 4*

Ingredients

1 large butternut squash
2 tbsp olive oil
½ tsp dried chilli flakes
Knob of ginger (approx. 5 cm)
1 large onion
1 litre vegetable stock
Salt and black pepper

Preparation method

Preheat the oven to 220°C and peel and deseed the squash before cutting into chunks.

Toss them with 1½ tbsp of the olive oil and place in a roasting tin.

Sprinkle with the chilli flakes and roast for 40–45 minutes until the squash is tender and the edges are starting to caramelise.

Meanwhile peel and grate the ginger and set aside.

In a large saucepan, heat the remaining oil and fry the onion (finely chopped) until translucent.

Add the roasted squash, grated ginger and the stock to the pan and simmer for 30 minutes.

Blend until smooth and season to taste.

Tip

Double the amount of chilli flakes for an extra kick.

COURGETTE SOUP

Quick. Easy. And satisfyingly green.

———————————————— *Serves 4* ————————————————

Ingredients

1 large onion

1 tbsp olive oil

2 small potatoes

2 large courgettes

*1 litre chicken or
vegetable stock*

Preparation method

Finely chop the onions. In a saucepan heat the oil and sauté them until soft.

Peel and dice the potatoes and roughly chop the courgettes, then add to the pan with the onions and stir well for another couple of minutes.

Add the stock and simmer for around 20 minutes until all the vegetables are cooked through.

Blend until smooth.

Serve piping hot with crusty bread.

CELERY SOUP

The perfect way to turn what is, for many, the villain of the vegetable world into a delicious, cheap and easy starter.

———————— ⊢ *Serves 4* ⊣ ————————

Ingredients

1 medium onion
1 medium potato
1 bunch of celery
Small knob of butter
1 tbsp olive oil

750 ml vegetable or
*   chicken stock*
100 ml crème fraiche
Salt and pepper

Preparation method

Prepare the vegetables: peel and chop the onion and potato and trim and dice the celery.

In a medium saucepan, heat the butter and the oil. Add the celery, onion and potato and cook gently for around 10 minutes, stirring regularly.

Add the stock and simmer for 20 minutes until all the vegetables are tender. Blend until smooth before stirring in the crème fraiche and adding seasoning to taste.

KALE SOUP

It might not win any beauty contests but there's no vegetable more in vogue than green, leafy kale. And it's healthy too – a superfood no less. Which is the perfect reason to turn it into this rich and appetising soup.

Serves 4

Ingredients

1 medium onion

2 cloves of garlic

3 small potatoes

2 tbsp butter

1 litre chicken or vegetable stock

400 g kale (rinsed)

Salt and pepper

4 tbsp sour cream to serve

Preparation method

Peel and finely chop the onion, peel and crush the garlic cloves and peel and dice the potatoes.

Heat the butter and fry the onion until soft but not browned.

Mix in the garlic and cook for another minute.

Stir in the diced potatoes then add the stock.

Bring to the boil and simmer until the potatoes are cooked through (around 10–15 minutes).

Roughly shred the kale, removing any thick, woody stems.

Add the kale and cook for 5–10 minutes before blending until smooth and adjusting the seasoning as necessary.

Serve topped with the sour cream.

Tip

Cavolo nero works well in place of the kale.

"

SOUPS WE GREW UP WITH.
SOUPS LIKE MAMMA USED
TO MAKE. SOUPS THAT UNITE
GENERATIONS IN COLLECTIVE
RAPTURE OVER A STEAMING
BOWL OF DELICIOUSNESS.

"

CLASSIC SOUPS

CREAM OF TOMATO SOUP

Will any soup ever topple cream of tomato from the top of the popularity lists? It's unlikely. Very unlikely indeed.

———————————— | *Serves 4–6* | ————————————

Ingredients

700 g fresh tomatoes, or 2 x 400 g tins of chopped tomatoes

2 tbsp cooking oil (vegetable or olive)

1 large onion

1.2 litres chicken or vegetable stock

Salt and pepper

100 ml single cream

Preparation method

If you are using fresh tomatoes, first remove the skins and the stems, then chop them finely. The best way of peeling a tomato is to score the fruit to break the skin, then place them in a bowl, pour boiling water over them and leave them to stand for a few minutes. Remove the tomatoes from the water and peel off the skins.

Heat the oil on a low heat in a large saucepan. Peel and chop the onion, then gently fry until it's softened.

Add the tomatoes, stock and seasoning, bring to the boil briefly, then reduce the heat and simmer for 15 minutes. Cool slightly then blitz until smooth. Stir in the cream and reheat gently before serving.

CARROT AND GINGER SOUP

A great way to use up all those carrots languishing at the bottom of the vegetable drawer. The mainstay of the 1980s dinner party, this might not be the coolest soup on the block, but decades later it still tastes great.

Serves 4–6

Ingredients

1 medium potato

750 g carrots

4-cm piece of fresh ginger

1.2 litres vegetable stock

Salt and pepper

Preparation method

Peel and chop the potatoes and carrots, and peel and grate the ginger.

Place the carrots, potato and ginger into a pan and cover with the stock. Bring to the boil and then simmer for 20 minutes.

Remove from the heat and either transfer the ingredients into a blender or use a stick blender. Blend until a smooth consistency is achieved. Season according to taste.

PEA SOUP

Simple, stunning and quick. There's no better way to eat your greens.

 Serves 4

Ingredients

1 onion

Knob of butter or 1 tbsp of olive oil

900 g frozen peas

900 ml vegetable stock (made from cube/ powder is fine)

Salt and pepper

Preparation method

Chop the onion then, in a large pan, sauté until softened but not browned.

Add the peas and the stock.

Boil for 3 or 4 minutes – any more and you may lose the vibrant bright green colour. Blend until smooth.

Season to taste and serve as is or with a swirl of crème fraiche and a garnish of chopped mint.

PUMPKIN SOUP

The ultimate Halloween feast, making the most of seasonal (and delicious) ingredients. Perfect for a spooky supper. Ghoulies and ghosties not required.

Serves 6

Ingredients

1.5 kg pumpkin

2 medium onions

50 ml olive oil

750 ml–1 litre vegetable or chicken stock

Salt and pepper

Toasted pumpkin seeds to garnish (optional)

Preparation method

Peel, deseed and chop the pumpkin into large chunks.

Peel and chop the onions then, in a large pan, heat the oil and gently fry until soft.

Add the pumpkin chunks and stock, bring to the boil and then cover and simmer until the pumpkin is tender.

Blend until smooth, season and simmer for a further 30 minutes.

Tip

Serve in a hollowed-out pumpkin for added wow factor.

COCK-A-LEEKIE

A name that always will always make small children giggle. Known as Scotland's national soup, this classic mix of chicken and leeks is hard to beat on a winter's day.

———————————— *Serves 6–8* ————————————

Ingredients

400 g leeks

1 x 2-kg chicken (a boiling fowl with giblets is best if you can get hold of one)

3 litres chicken stock

1 bouquet garni

30 g long-grain rice (optional)

Salt and pepper

Preparation method

Trim and slice the leeks.

Place the chicken in a large saucepan, together with the stock, leeks and bouquet garni.

Bring to the boil, removing any scum or froth from the surface.

Turn the heat right down and simmer gently for 2 hours, adding a little more water if the level drops.

Remove the chicken from the pot and cut up as much meat as you'd like in the soup (no skin).

Add the meat to the stock along with the rice.

Simmer for 20–30 minutes, adjusting the seasoning as needed.

Tip

Original recipes for cock-a-leekie featured prunes. For an authentic version, soak 10 prunes in water overnight and add at the same time as the rice.

"

FOR WHEN YOU NEED A
PICK-ME-UP – A PERFECT
GASTRONOMIC HUG
WHEN YOU'RE NOT
FEELING 100 PER CENT.

"

SOOTHING
SOUPS

THICK LEEK AND POTATO SOUP

With crusty bread and lots of golden butter, there's nothing quite as comforting as this familiar favourite. Grab a bowl… aaaaand relax.

———————————— *Serves 4–6* ————————————

Ingredients

1 large onion
2 medium potatoes
2 leeks
2 tbsp olive oil
1.2 litres chicken or vegetable stock
Salt and pepper
150 ml double cream or crème fraiche (optional)

Preparation method

Peel and chop the onion and potatoes, and wash, trim and slice the leeks.

Heat the oil in a large pan and gently fry the onions, potatoes and leeks for 3–4 minutes until they start to soften; stir from time to time.

Add the stock and bring to the boil, then reduce heat and simmer until the vegetables are tender.

Season to taste.

Leave to cool then blitz until smooth.

Add the cream, if you like, and serve hot.

FRENCH ONION SOUP

The very definition of comfort food. Rich, warming *and* with stringy, cheesy bits on top.

Serves 4–6

Ingredients

750 g onions
50 g butter
1 tbsp olive oil
1 tsp sugar
2 cloves garlic
2 tbsp plain flour
250 ml dry white wine

50 ml brandy or sherry
  (optional)
1.25 litres beef stock

For the topping:

1 baguette
150 g grated Gruyère

Preparation method

Thinly slice the onions. Melt the butter with the oil in a large saucepan, then add the onions and fry gently until soft.

Add the sugar and cook until the onions caramelise (around 15–20 minutes), stirring often to prevent them sticking/burning.

Crush the garlic, add to the pan and cook for a further couple of minutes.

Mix in the flour then turn up the heat before adding the wine (stir as you do this).

At this stage you should add the sherry or brandy if using.

Pour in the stock then cover and simmer for 20 minutes. Meanwhile prepare the croutons by slicing the baguette into thick slices, lightly brushing each slice with olive oil and cooking on a griddle pan until lightly toasted.

Ladle the soup into bowls, add the croutons and then sprinkle with the Gruyère. Place under a hot grill until the cheese starts to bubble.

Tip

To make a vegetarian version, simply replace the beef stock with vegetable stock. And do make sure you use bowls that will withstand the heat of the grill!

MATZO BALL SOUP

This is Jewish penicillin, the cure for all ills (be they physical or emotional). There are versions aplenty, but all have the magical properties… and the magical taste.

Serves 4–6

Ingredients

For the soup:

1 large onion

3 medium carrots

2 sticks of celery

1 chicken (a boiling fowl with giblets is best but a regular chicken will do)

2 tsp salt plus extra and black pepper to season

1–2 ripe tomatoes (optional)

For the matzo balls:

2 eggs

2 tbsp shmaltz (rendered chicken fat) or margarine

20 g ground almonds

130 g medium matzo meal

Salt and pepper

4 tbsp warm water

Preparation method

For the soup:

Peel the onion and chop in half, peel and chop the carrots and cut the celery into large pieces.

Put the chicken into a large saucepan. Add a couple of teaspoons of salt, a little black pepper and 2 litres of water.

Cover and bring to the boil, removing any froth or scum from the surface.

Add to the pan the vegetables (including the tomatoes, if using) and bring back to the boil before reducing the heat to a low simmer.

Cover the pan and cook for 2–3 hours until the chicken is tender.

Strain the soup, keeping the carrot and giblets in a separate bowl.

Cover and refrigerate overnight.

When you remove the soup from the fridge it will have thick yellow layer of fat on top. Remove this carefully and put the soup back into a pan and reheat. At this stage you can add the carrot and giblets (if you like). You can also keep back some onion when straining and add this too, for those who like it.

For the matzo balls:

Whisk the eggs.

Gently melt the shmaltz or margarine then stir in the eggs, almonds, meal and seasoning, together with 3–4 tbsp of warm water.

Mix thoroughly.

Chill until the mixture has firmed (at least an hour).

Divide the chilled mixture into walnut-sized pieces and roll into balls (wet hands prevent them from sticking).

The balls should be simmered for around 30 minutes before serving: drop them into a pan of lightly salted boiling water and then strain before adding to the soup just before serving, or cook in the chicken soup itself.

Tip

You can use the equivalent weight of chicken pieces instead of a whole bird. Thighs and legs work well.

If you can get hold of them, a neck (from your butcher) and any giblets will really help to bring out the flavour of the soup.

Another traditional accompaniment is lokshen, or noodles. This can be cooked in boiling water or in the soup itself – allow 10–20 g per person.

ROASTED RED PEPPER SOUP

Colour therapy! This is a sweet, vibrant soup, worth making for the glorious redness alone (though it tastes pretty good too).

Serves 4

Ingredients

3 large red peppers
500 g ripe tomatoes
1 large red onion
2–3 tbsp olive oil

4 cloves garlic
1 litre vegetable or chicken stock
Salt and pepper

Preparation method

Preheat the oven to 200°C.

Deseed the peppers, remove stalks and cut into quarters. Halve the tomatoes and peel and chop the onion.

Place the peppers and tomatoes (cut side up) in a large roasting tin. Drizzle with 1–2 tbsp olive oil.

Roast for 30–40 minutes until the edges are beginning to brown. Remove and leave to cool slightly.

Meanwhile, heat a tablespoon of olive oil in a saucepan and fry the onion until soft and browned.

Crush then add the garlic and cook for a further minute. Add the stock and bring to the boil before reducing to a gentle simmer.

When the peppers have cooled slightly, remove as much skin as you can (it doesn't matter if there's some left on) and add the peppers, tomatoes and any juices from the tin to the stock.

Simmer for 10–15 minutes, then blend until the vegetables are combined (it doesn't need to be silky smooth). Season to taste.

Serve with some fresh, chopped basil and a drizzle of olive oil (extra virgin is best).

Tip

Try adding a little good-quality balsamic vinegar with the basil and olive oil before serving.

"

CHILL OUT IN THE HEAT
WITH THE COOLEST
SOUPS AROUND.

"

REFRESHING SOUPS

GAZPACHO

Bring a little taste of Spain to your dining table with this classic chilled soup – there's nothing more refreshing on a hot, humid summer's day.

———————————| *Serves 4–6* |———————————

Ingredients

1 shallot

2 cloves garlic

1 medium cucumber

750–900 g ripe tomatoes

2 tbsp sherry vinegar

Salt and pepper

60 ml extra virgin olive oil

Garnishes – chopped cucumber, black olives, hard-boiled egg, red onion, spring onion, peppers, chopped parsley or basil all work well.

Preparation method

Peel and chop the shallot and the garlic.

Halve the cucumber lengthways and remove the seeds.

Roughly chop the tomatoes, discarding any tough cores.

Blend the tomatoes until fine, then add the rest of the vegetables, blending again until they form a thick liquid.

Mix in the vinegar and ½ tsp salt (you may want to add more at the tasting stage).

Gradually blend in the olive oil then season, adding pepper and any further salt or vinegar to taste.

Refrigerate until fully chilled.

Tip

If you can, make the soup the day before you need it. This helps the flavours to infuse.

Add ice cubes to the serving bowl before serving – it helps keep the soup really cold and adds an authentic touch.

BORSCHT

No soup does variations on a theme better than the Eastern European staple that is borscht. Hot, cold, thick, thin, with sausage, with cream… and not – shock horror – always made with beetroot (though in our book the best versions are – always).

──────────── ┤ *Serves 4* ├ ────────────

Ingredients

1 kg beets
2 large carrots
1 large onion
1.5 litres chicken or vegetable stock
2 garlic cloves
1 tbsp sugar
Salt and pepper

Preparation method

Peel the vegetables and roughly dice into pieces approximately 2 cm in diameter.

Add, with the stock and the peeled garlic, to a large pan with the sugar and cook until the vegetables are tender and the liquid a dark, vibrant red.

Blend the soup until smooth and then pass through a medium sieve.

Season to taste.

Serve chilled, with a dollop of sour cream.

Tip

This works best when it's made the day before it's eaten as this allows time for the flavours to fully infuse.

It can be reheated gently before serving, traditionally with a garnish of sliced boiled potato.

CUCUMBER SOUP

When is a salad not a salad? Simple… when it's a
delicious and impressive chilled summer soup.

———————————— *Serves 4* ————————————

Ingredients

1 medium potato

3 cucumbers

4 spring onions

Knob of butter

1 litre vegetable stock

1 small gem or cos lettuce

100 ml double cream or crème fraiche

Salt and pepper

Chopped chives or shredded mint leaves to garnish

Preparation method

Peel and roughly chop the potato. Peel, seed and
roughly chop the cucumber. Slice the spring onions.

In a saucepan melt the butter and sauté the spring onions until soft.

Add the potatoes and stock and simmer for around 20 minutes until the potatoes are cooked through.
Add the cucumber and the shredded lettuce and simmer for a further 15 minutes.

Allow the soup to cool slightly before using a stick blender to puree until smooth.

Stir in the cream or crème fraiche, season and allow to cool before chilling.

Serve with chopped chives or shredded mint leaves.

MELON SOUP

Continuing our theme... when is a soup not a starter? When it's a dessert of course. And a light, refreshing, summery one at that.

———————————— *Serves 4* ————————————

Ingredients

1 honeydew melon
Juice of 1 lime

Caster sugar (optional)
2 tbsp fresh chopped mint

Preparation method

Remove the skin and seeds from the melon and cut the flesh into chunks. Blend with the lime juice to form a smooth puree.

Add sugar to taste (if the melon is very sweet you might not need any). Stir in the mint leaves and serve chilled.

Tip

If using smaller melons, try scooping out the flesh and using the peel as a bowl to serve the soup.

VICHYSSOISE

Vichyssoise (which sounds far more exciting than 'cold leek and potato soup') is an easy way to impress guests at a summer dinner party.

Serves 4

Ingredients

1 medium onion
500 g leeks
50 g butter
1 medium potato

750 ml chicken or
*   vegetable stock*
100 ml double cream
Salt and pepper

Preparation method

Peel and chop the onion and slice the leeks finely. In a medium saucepan melt the butter and cook together until soft (around 10 minutes).

Peel and chop the potato and add to the pan together with the stock. Simmer for 20–30 minutes until the potatoes are tender.

Blend the soup until smooth, then add the cream and seasoning to taste and mix to combine fully. Serve chilled.

"

GLOBAL GORGEOUSNESS
FROM MOROCCO TO MEXICO,
TAKING IN THE BEST OF
THE ORIENT EN ROUTE.

"

SOUPS FROM AROUND THE WORLD

HOT AND SOUR SOUP (TOM YUM)

Spicy and sour, this is a detox in a dish and is even said to ward off colds. The flavours of Thailand… without having to buy a plane ticket.

———————— | *Serves 4* | ————————

Ingredients

4 small red or green chillies

3 stalks lemongrass

3-cm piece of galangal (Chinese ginger)

8 kaffir lime leaves

1.5 litres chicken stock

500 ml water

2 tbsp palm sugar

3 tbsp fish sauce

Juice of 1½ limes

20 small raw prawns (peeled and de-veined)

Spring onion and coriander to garnish

Preparation method

Finely chop the chillies, bruise the lemongrass stalks and cut into pieces, peel and slice the galangal, and bruise and tear the lime leaves.

In a medium saucepan, heat the stock and the water.

Add the galangal, lime leaves and lemongrass and bring to the boil.

Reduce the heat and simmer for 10 minutes.

Add the chillies and simmer for a further 5 minutes before adding the sugar, fish sauce and lime juice.

Tip in the prawns and continue cooking until they're pink (around 2–3 minutes).

Serve garnished with finely sliced spring onions and coriander leaves.

Tip

If you can't get hold of galangal, you can replace it with root ginger. And if you can't find palm sugar, use soft brown or caster sugar instead. You can also add small chunks of raw chicken breast to the soup a couple of minutes before adding the prawns. Makes sure they are cooked through before serving.

CHICKEN AND SWEETCORN SOUP

Gorgeously glutinous, this quick and easy version of the Chinese favourite beats a takeaway any day.

———————————————| *Serves 4* |———————————————

Ingredients

2 tbsp cornflour
1 litre chicken stock
200 g cooked, shredded chicken breast (no skin)
2 small tins of sweetcorn
2 eggs
Soy sauce

Preparation method

Mix the cornflour with a little chicken stock to form a smooth paste and set aside.

Heat the rest of the stock in a medium pan, then add the chicken and the (drained) sweetcorn.

Bring to the boil, then reduce to a simmer and gradually add the cornflour paste, stirring until the soup begins to thicken.

Bring to the boil again, beat the eggs then add gradually, stirring constantly to break them into strands.

Season with soy sauce and serve garnished with spring onions.

Tip

You can use a tin of creamed sweetcorn in place of the two small tins of regular corn.

MISO SOUP

Low in calories, high in protein, minerals and antioxidants – this light and simple Japanese staple is hailed by many as a superfood. Or should that be soup-erfood?

———————— ┤ *Serves 4* ├ ————————

Ingredients

2 x 8 g sachets of dashi*

750 ml water

2 tbsp miso paste

2 spring onions

1 tbsp dried nori or wakame seaweed (optional)

1 tbsp mirin

½ pack firm tofu

*Dashi is a stock used in many Japanese recipes. It is usually made from kelp (seaweed) or bonito flakes (dried fish).

Preparation method

Mix the dashi and water together in a medium saucepan and bring to the boil.

Reduce to a simmer and take a ladle of the stock and mix with the miso in a small bowl or jug to form a smooth, thick liquid (this stops the soup becoming lumpy).

Finely slice the spring onions then add, with the seaweed, to the pan and simmer gently for a couple of minutes, before adding the miso mixture and the mirin, stirring continually.

Cut the tofu into small cubes, add to the soup and heat gently – don't allow it to boil – before serving.

Tip

If you can't find dashi, you can use a tablespoon of good-quality vegetable stock powder instead.

PHO

A traditional Vietnamese noodle soup, which can be served with beef, chicken, seafood or vegetables. Oh, and you pronounce it *fuh*. Not *foe* (as I have done in error – more than once).

─────── *Serves 4* ───────

Ingredients

4-cm piece root ginger

2 cloves of garlic

4 spring onions

2 litres hot beef stock

2 cloves

2 star anise

1 tsp black peppercorns

1 cinnamon stick

400 g rice noodles

200 g beef sirloin or flank

150 g bean sprouts

3 tbsp fish sauce

1–2 red chillies to serve (depending how hot you like it)

Small bunch fresh coriander

1 lime

Preparation method

Peel and slice the ginger, crush the garlic and trim and slice the spring onions.

Simmer the stock, together with the onion, ginger, garlic, spices and cinnamon stick, covered, for 45 minutes.

Cook the noodles (according to the instructions on the packet) and divide between 4 serving bowls.

Finely slice the raw beef, divide between the bowls and place onto noodles. Then add the beansprouts.

Drain the stock then return to the pan, adding the fish sauce and heating gently.

Ladle the hot stock over the noodles, meat and beansprouts.

Serve with chopped chilli, coriander, sliced spring onions and a wedge of lime, along with hoisin or chilli sauce.

Tip

Freeze the beef for 15 minutes to make it firmer and easier to slice thinly. Once cut, keep refrigerated until ready to serve.

MOROCCAN CHICKPEA SOUP

The combination of spices and citrus brings a unique flavour to this chunky soup that takes just minutes to make.

———————————————— ⊢ *Serves 4* ⊢ ————————————————

Ingredients

1 large onion
2 cloves of garlic
250 g chickpeas or 1 x 400 g can of chickpeas
2 tbsp olive oil
1 tsp cinnamon
2 tsp ground cumin
1 tsp chilli powder
2 tbsp tomato puree
750 ml vegetable stock
Juice of half a lemon or lime
Salt and pepper
Fresh coriander to serve

Preparation method

Peel and finely chop the onion and crush the garlic.

Drain the chickpeas.

In a saucepan, heat the olive oil and fry the onion until soft but not browned.

Add the garlic and the spices and fry for another minute.

Add the tomato puree, stock and chickpeas and simmer for 10–15 minutes until the flavours have combined.

Adjust the seasoning, stir in the lemon or lime juice and serve garnished with chopped coriander.

Tip

For a deeper, richer flavour, try adding a tin of chopped tomatoes.

CHICKEN LAKSA

The laksa's fame has spread from Malaysia, Indonesia and Singapore – and rightly so. The combination of rice noodles, spices and chicken (or prawns) makes this the perfect main-meal soup.

—————————| *Serves 4* |—————————

Ingredients

2 red chillies

3 cloves of garlic

4-cm piece of root ginger

2 shallots

2 stalks of lemongrass

Small handful of coriander leaves (plus extra for serving)

2 tsp turmeric

1 tbsp vegetable oil

1 x 400 ml can coconut milk

400 ml chicken stock

2 boneless, skinless chicken breasts

1 tsp palm (or caster) sugar (optional)

2 tbsp fish sauce

150g fine rice noodles

1 lime

Preparation method

Deseed and roughly chop the chillies, peel the garlic, peel and roughly chop the ginger and shallots and chop the lemon grass into pieces.

Put these ingredients, together with the coriander, turmeric and vegetable oil, into a small food processor and blend to form a smooth paste.

In a wok (or saucepan) gently fry the paste for a minute or two, stirring to release the flavours.

Add the coconut milk and the stock. Bring to the boil before reducing to a simmer. Cut the chicken into small pieces and add to the pan with the sugar (if using) and the fish sauce.

Continue to simmer for 8–10 minutes or until the chicken is cooked through.

Cook the rice noodles according to the packet instructions. Drain and divide them between the four bowls.

Ladle the soup over the top, making sure that the chicken is divided evenly between the bowls. Serve with chopped coriander and a wedge of lime.

"

THICK, FILLING AND
HEARTY – THESE SOUPS
ARE THE PERFECT FUEL FOR
A BUSY DAY OR WARDING
OFF CHILLY WEATHER.

"

HEARTY
SOUPS

MINESTRONE SOUP

Dating back to Roman times, this chunky Italian mix of beans, tomatoes and whatever vegetables you happen to have hanging around makes the perfect budget supper.

⊢ *Serves 4* ⊢

Ingredients

1 large onion

2 large carrots

1 medium potato

3 celery sticks

1 garlic clove

¼ of a green cabbage

1 tbsp olive oil

1 x 400 g can chopped tomatoes

2 tbsp tomato puree

1.5 litres vegetable or chicken stock

1 x 400 g can cannellini beans

100 g small pasta shapes

1 tsp dried oregano

Salt and pepper

Parmesan to serve

Preparation method

Peel and finely chop the onion and carrots and potato. Finely chop the celery, crush the garlic and finely shred the cabbage.

In a large pan heat the olive oil and cook the onion, carrot and celery until soft. Add the garlic and fry for a further minute or two.

Mix in the potato, the tinned tomatoes, the tomato puree and the stock and simmer for around 10 minutes, until the potato is starting to soften.

Add the beans, the pasta and any other diced vegetables you are using and simmer for a further 10 minutes before stirring in the shredded cabbage.

Cook for two minutes then season.

Serve topped with freshly grated Parmesan.

Tip

You can vary the vegetables according to what you have to use up. Courgettes, green beans and peas all work well. Note that if you add more veg you may also need to increase the amount of stock. If you can't find small pasta shapes you can use regular spaghetti snapped into short lengths, or macaroni.

BEAN AND BARLEY SOUP

Another hearty vegetable soup that's almost a meal in itself. Low fat, high fibre – you can practically see the halo.

—————————— *Serves 4* ——————————

Ingredients

1 medium onion

1 carrot

1 stick celery

2 tbsp olive oil

200 g pearl barley

2 x 400 g cans of
    cannellini beans
    (drained and rinsed)

1 litre vegetable stock

Salt and pepper

Preparation method

Peel and finely chop the onion and carrots. Finely chop the celery, discarding any leaves. In a saucepan, heat the oil and fry the onion, carrot and celery until they start to soften.

Add the barley, beans and stock, stir well, cover and simmer for around 45 minutes, or until the barley is cooked. Stir regularly to prevent it from sticking. If you prefer your soup to be slightly thinner, you can add a little more water. Season to taste.

CARROT AND LENTIL SOUP

This soup is packed with fibre and protein – and it's filling and delicious to boot. Serve with thick slices of buttered toast. Can there be a finer winter lunch?

Serves 4

Ingredients

1 large onion

4 carrots

200 g red lentils

1 tbsp olive oil

2 litres vegetable stock (fresh or made with 2 cubes)

Salt and pepper

Preparation method

Peel and chop the onion and carrots and rinse the lentils. Heat the oil in a large saucepan and fry the onion until it starts to soften. Add the carrots and mix well.

Pour in the hot stock, add the lentils then cover and simmer for 15–20 minutes until the lentils are soft.

Remove from the heat and blend. Note that it doesn't need to be silky smooth and the odd lump of carrot isn't a problem. Season to taste.

CULLEN SKINK

Fish soup, Scottish style. What better way to warm your cockles? (Pun absolutely intended.)

———————— ┤ *Serves 4* ├————————

Ingredients

1 medium onion
2 medium potatoes
1 tbsp olive oil or butter
300 ml boiling water
400 g undyed smoked haddock (skinned)
300 ml milk
Salt and pepper
Chopped chives to serve

Preparation method

Peel and finely chop the onion. Peel and dice the potatoes.

In a medium saucepan, heat the oil and fry the onion until soft but not browned.

Add the potatoes and the water and cook for around 15 minutes until tender.

Meanwhile, poach the haddock in the milk for around 7 minutes until cooked through. Remove from the pan – reserving the liquid – and break up into large flakes, ensuring any bones are removed.

Roughly mash the potatoes, still in the liquid, then add the milk and fish to the pan.

Heat through and season.

Serve garnished with chopped chives.

SCOTCH BROTH

Dating back centuries, this traditional potage is more main meal than starter, and so warming that it's probably as close as you'll get to a hot-water bottle in liquid form.

———————— *Serves 6–8* ————————

Ingredients

200 g carrots

1 small swede or turnip

*1 large onion
(or 2 medium)*

1 leek

200 g cabbage

Curly parsley to garnish

500 g lamb (on the bone)

2 litres water

200 g potatoes

100 g pearl barley

Salt and pepper

Preparation method

Peel and dice the carrots, swede or turnip, and onion.

Trim, clean and slice the leeks. Shred the cabbage. Chop the parsley (leaves only) and set aside to garnish.

Put the lamb and the water into a large pan, ensuring the lamb is covered – you can add more water if needed, and simmer for half an hour, removing any scum that forms on the surface. There will be quite a lot – this is normal!

Add the swede or turnip, along with the potato, carrots, onion, leek and cabbage. Simmer over a very low heat for around an hour, by which time the meat and the vegetables should be tender. Remove any further froth as needed.

Carefully remove the meat from the pot and allow it to cool.

Meanwhile, add the barley and continue to simmer for around 30 minutes.

Remove all the meat from the lamb bones and add to the pot, simmering for a further 15–20 minutes until the barley is tender, stirring regularly to prevent it sticking. Continue to remove any scum or fat from the top with a large spoon.

Season to taste and stir in the parsley.

Tip

As long, slow cooking is the key, this works well in a slow cooker.

> **IDEAL FOR ENTERTAINING, WHEN YOU WANT TO SERVE YOUR GUESTS SOMETHING SPECIAL.**

FANCY SOUPS

AVOCADO SOUP

Avocado. In a salad, served with vinaigrette, or as a chunky guacamole. For sure. But as a soup? Oh yes. Prepare to be converted.

Serves 4

Ingredients

1 medium onion
3 garlic cloves
1 tbsp olive oil
2 ripe avocados

2 tbsp lime juice
600 ml chicken or
   vegetable stock
Salt and pepper

Preparation method

Peel and chop the onion and garlic. Heat the oil and gently cook the onion until soft but not browned. Add the garlic and cook for another minute.

Stone, peel and mash the avocados and mix with the lime juice to prevent them from browning.

Put the cooked vegetables, avocados and stock into a food processor and blend until smooth. Season to taste and serve chilled.

BROCCOLI AND STILTON SOUP

Smooth, velvety and sophisticated – yet incredibly quick and easy to make. Fast food takes on a whole new meaning.

Serves 4

Ingredients

1 medium onion

500 g broccoli

1 tbsp olive oil

100 g Stilton

Salt and pepper

Preparation method

Peel and finely chop the onion and roughly chop the broccoli.

In a medium saucepan, heat the oil and fry the onion until soft but not browned. Stir in the broccoli and cook for a further minute.

Add the stock and simmer for 5–7 minutes or until the broccoli is tender.

Crumble then add half the Stilton and blend until smooth. Serve with the remainder of the cheese crumbled on top.

SEAFOOD CHOWDER

Creamy, rich and utterly luxurious: a fish pie in soup form. Crusty bread for mopping up is essential.

─────────────── *Serves 4* ───────────────

Ingredients

1 large onion

2 medium potatoes

2 stalks celery

1 tbsp vegetable oil or butter

2 tbsp plain flour

1 fish stock cube

500 ml water

500 ml milk

1 bay leaf

A pinch of cayenne pepper

Salt and pepper

600 g fish (you can use raw skinless fillets such as salmon, smoked haddock and firm white fish (e.g. cod, haddock), a mix of cooked shellfish or ideally a combination of the two)

100 ml single cream

Chopped parsley to serve

Preparation method

Peel and dice the onion and potatoes and dice the celery.

In a large saucepan, heat the butter or oil and cook the onion and celery for ten minutes or until soft.

Stir in the flour and cook for a further minute before gradually adding the fish stock, stirring well.

Add the milk, the bay leaf, the cayenne, salt and pepper, then cover and simmer for 10 minutes, or until the potatoes are cooked through.

Meanwhile, prepare the raw fish by removing any skin or bones and chopping into small chunks, around 2 cm.

When the potatoes are cooked, add the fish to the pan and simmer gently for 4 minutes.

Add any cooked shellfish, together with the cream, then simmer for another minute.

Serve immediately, sprinkled with the chopped parsley.

WATERCRESS SOUP

Subtle and elegant – a perfect choice for dinner parties
and smart suppers.

———————— Serves 4 ————————

Ingredients

1 small onion
2 medium potatoes (around 350 g)
1 tbsp olive oil
750 ml chicken or vegetable stock
275 g fresh watercress
150 ml milk
Salt and pepper
Pinch freshly grated nutmeg (optional)

Preparation method

Peel and chop the onion and peel and dice the potatoes.

Heat the oil in a large pan and gently cook the onion
until soft.

Add the potato and stock and simmer for 10–15 minutes until the potatoes are cooked through.
Remove any tough stalks from the watercress then add to the pan and simmer for a further 2 or 3 minutes (until the watercress is wilted).

Take off the heat and blend until smooth.

Add the milk, the seasoning and the nutmeg. Stir and heat gently before serving.

Tip

For a richer and thicker soup, you can replace the milk with double cream.

ASPARAGUS SOUP

Make the most of the asparagus season with this simple yet sophisticated starter. It takes only minutes to make (you just don't need to tell your guests that).

———————————| *Serves 4* |———————————

Ingredients

500 g asparagus
3 shallots
Knob of butter
700 ml vegetable or chicken stock
6 tbsp crème fraiche or double cream
Salt and pepper

Preparation method

Remove the woody ends of the asparagus then chop the rest into 2-cm pieces. Peel and finely chop the shallots.

Melt the butter in a medium saucepan and cook the shallots until translucent – don't allow them to brown.

Add the asparagus and cook for a further 3 minutes, stirring to prevent sticking/browning.

Pour in the stock and simmer until the asparagus is tender – around 20 minutes.

Blend the soup until smooth, stir in the cream or crème fraiche and season.

Reheat gently to serve (don't allow it to boil).

Tip

This also works beautifully as a cold soup. After adding the cream, simply chill until time to serve.

ARTICHOKE SOUP

This is actually a bit of an imposter; it might sound sophisticated, but this sweet and nutty soup really couldn't be simpler.

———————————— *Serves 4* ————————————

Ingredients

1 medium onion
100 g potato
600 g Jerusalem artichokes
1 garlic clove
1 tbsp olive oil
Splash of white wine (optional)
750 ml chicken or vegetable stock
100 ml double cream
Salt and pepper

Preparation method

Peel and chop the onion and potato, peel and slice the artichokes and crush the garlic.

In a medium saucepan heat the oil and cook the onion gently until soft but not browned.

Add the garlic and cook for another minute.

If using the wine, add now and bring to the boil.

Stir in the stock, the artichokes and the potatoes and reduce to a simmer.

Cook for 15–20 minutes or until the vegetables are soft.

Blend until smooth, stirring in the cream and seasoning.

Heat through gently and serve.

Tip

For a creamier soup you can add more cream or replace some of the stock with milk.

If you're interested in finding out more
about our books, find us on Facebook
at **Summersdale Publishers** and follow
us on Twitter at **@Summersdale**.

Thanks very much for buying
this Summersdale book.

www.summersdale.com